Heartsongs

W9-CMC-150

CONTENTS

TRACK LISTING DEFINITIONS

(1) This symbol indicates an accompaniment track number on the StudioTrax CD.

(33) This symbol indicates a split track number on the StudioTrax CD.

MarkFoster MUSIC

A DIVISION OF SHAWNEE PRESS, INC.

EXCLUSIVELY DISTRIBUTED BY HAL LEONARD CORPORATION

Visit Shawnee Press Online at

www.shawneepress.com

HEARTSONGS

FOREWORD

"Heartsongs" is a song cycle inspired by the life and words of the amazing young poet, Mattie J.T. Stepanek. (See biography on page 3.) Through his poetry and personal appearances, Mattie impacted the world with an authenticity of spirit rarely seen.

There are eight choral songs in the cycle, and they represent some of the important elements of Mattie's writing. Six of the movements are based on actual poems written by Mattie. Two of the movements are my personal "Heartsongs," with original texts that connect to specific aspects of Mattie's message. In his first book Mattie left blank pages for people to write their own "Heartsongs." These songs may be sung as a complete cycle or may be performed individually. An optional narration is also included.

In between the songs you can read Mattie's poems as he wrote them. Simple, and yet profound in their insights, these lines are treasured testimonies of the human spirit, and gentle admonitions for us to listen and learn.

It is essential to have young voices sing this music. It is their "Heartsongs" that can truly change the world and bring Mattie's dreams for a better world to glorious reality.

JOSEPH M. MARTIN

Mattie J.T. Stepanek, a well-respected poet and peace activist, lived a life that was brief in length but powerfully blessed with depth. Born on July 17, 1990, Mattie began creating and sharing "Heartsongs" at the young age of 3. He explained that Heartsongs are "gifts that reflect each person's unique reason for being." Mattie ultimately published six collections of his "Heartsongs" poetry books and one collection of "Just Peace" essays and e-mail correspondence between Mattie and Former President Jimmy Carter. All seven of Mattie's books became New York Times Bestsellers and touched millions of lives around the world. Mattie gave inspirational speeches to a variety of audiences; was a frequent guest on shows like Oprah, Larry King Live, and Good Morning America; and he served as a three-term National Goodwill Ambassador for the Muscular Dystrophy Association. His philosophy for life was "Remember to play after every storm!" and he wanted to be remembered as "a poet, a peacemaker, and a philosopher who played." Mattie died on June 22, 2004 due to complications of the rare neuromuscular disease that caused him to rely on a ventilator and wheelchair much of his life. Since his death, numerous parks, libraries, peace programs, and awards have been named in his honor, and many schools are using Mattie's writings and his message of hope and peace as an educational and motivational tool for teaching students. Recently, Mattie's mom, Jeni, penned "Messenger: The Legacy of Mattie J.T. Stepanek and Heartsongs." The memoir offers the intimate details of this ordinary child who lived an extraordinary life by making choices that celebrated life to its fullest even during the darkest challenges, and in doing so, inspired others to do the same. For more information visit **www.mattieonline.com.**

Poem: HEARTSONG
by Mattie J.T. Stepanek
March, 1996
in "Journey Through Heartsongs" (Hyperion, 2002)

I have a song, deep in my heart,
And only I can hear it.
If I close my eyes and sit very still
It is so easy to listen to my song.
When my eyes are open and
I am so busy and moving and busy,
If I take time to listen very hard,
I can still hear my Heartsong.
It makes me feel happy.
Happier than ever.
Happier than everywhere
And everything and everyone
In the whole wide world.
Happy like thinking about
Going to Heaven when I die.
My Heartsong sounds like this -
    I love you! I love you!
    How happy you can be!
    How happy you can make
    This whole world be!
And sometimes it's other
Tunes and words, too,
But it always sings the
Same special feeling to me.
It makes me think of
Jamie, and Katie and Stevie,
And other wonderful things.
This is my special song.
But do you know what?
All people have a special song
Inside their hearts!
Everyone in the whole wide world
Has a special Heartsong.
If you believe in magical, musical hearts,
And if you believe you can be happy,
Then you, too, will hear your song.

HEARTSONG

Words based on the poem
"Heartsong" *by*
MATTIE J.T. STEPANEK
March, 1996
in "Journey Through Heartsongs" (Hyperion, 2002)

Music by
JOSEPH M. MARTIN (BMI)

6

HEARTSONGS

beau-ti-ful things; and I want to share it with you.

beau-ti-ful things; and I want to share it with you.

It's so won-der-ful! It's so mag-i-cal! Let the mu-sic be-

It's so won-der-ful! It's so mag-i-cal! Let the mu-sic be-

gin. Lis-ten to your heart-song._____ Lis-ten to your

gin. It's the mu-sic of love_____ and peace.

10

INTRODUCTION:

The lyrics and music of "Heartsongs" reflect the hopeful message of an extraordinary young man, Mattie J.T. Stepanek. Challenged by a rare but fatal form of muscular dystrophy Mattie's courage and grace inspired millions through his writing. He wrote with eloquent simplicity poetry he called "Heartsongs." He chronicled about his dreams for life, his hopes for the world and his prayers for peace. His writing awakened in the hearts of many the music of grace, joy and love. As Mattie once put it… "A Heartsong is an inner message. It is a person's inner beauty and reason for being. It is what we need and want most in life… that is what we are called to offer others."

Even with all Mattie endured in his daily life he remained joyful and hopeful. He treasured the relationships of family and friends. He relished holidays and the changing of the seasons. With honesty and authenticity he poured out his heart into his pen. These testaments of hope are reminders for us all to treasure the moments we are given. Hear now Mattie's encouraging poem "Enter the Season."

Poem: ENTER THE SEASON
by Mattie J.T. Stepanek
December, 2000
in "Reflections of a Peacemaker" (Andrews McMeel, 2005)

> *The season is upon us now,*
> *Let us enter, here is how…*
>
> *Come in joy to celebrate.*
> *Come in hope for future's sake.*
> *Come in gently, open-hearted.*
> *Come for unborn and departed.*
> *Come in happiness and mirth.*
> *Come with faith that serves the earth.*
> *Come in kindness, come forgiving.*
> *Come to share the gift of living.*
> *Come in patient, calm, assuring.*
> *Come with grace and trust enduring.*
> *But most of all, let's come in peace,*
> *The dark of angry hurt, release.*
>
> *The season 'tis upon us now,*
> *As we enter, let us vow…*
>
> *For young and old in every land,*
> *Let us come joined hand-in-hand.*

14

ENTER THE SEASON

Words based on the poem
"Enter the Season" *by*
MATTIE J.T. STEPANEK
December, 2000
in "Reflections of a Peacemaker" (Andrews McMeel, 2005)

Music by
JOSEPH M. MARTIN (BMI)

fu - ture's sake.__ Come in joy to cel - e - brate.__

fu - ture's sake.__ Come__ in__ joy to cel - e - brate.__

Come in hope;__ lift__ high your praise!__

Come in hope;__ lift__ high your praise!__

27 PARTS I & II
mp *unis.*   *mf*

Come in, gent - ly o - pen - heart - ed. Come for un - born

Come in pa - tient,_ calm, as - sur - ing. Come with grace and_

trust en - dur - ing. The dark of an - gry_ hurt re - lease;

PART I

and most of all,_____ and

PART II

and most of all,_ and

24

Come for un - born and de - part - ed.

Come for un - born and de - part - ed.

Come in hap - pi - ness and mirth.

Come in hap - pi - ness and mirth.

Come with faith that serves the earth.

Come with faith that serves— the— earth.

26

Come with grace and_ trust en - dur - ing. The dark of an - gry

Come with grace and_ trust en - dur - ing. The dark of an - gry_

hurt re - lease, and most of all,_____

hurt re - lease, and

and most of all,_____ let's come in

most of all,___ and most of all,___

Because of Mattie's unusual insight on the world and his unique ability to communicate his thoughts through his writing, it is sometimes easy to forget that he was a young boy. Some of his writing helps us to remember the joyful child in us all. Inspired by friendships and the glory of a beautiful summer day he wrote "Butterfly Summer."

Poem: BUTTERFLY SUMMER
by Mattie J.T. Stepanek
August, 1998
in "Celebrate Through Heartsongs" (Hyperion, 2002)

This was a summer.
A Butterfly Summer.
A time and sign,
Of peace, grace, and
Happiness.
Beautiful rainbows of
So many colors, of
Rainbow butterflies
This was a Summer,
A Butterfly Summer.

BUTTERFLY SUMMER

Words based on the poem
"Butterfly Summer" *by*
MATTIE J.T. STEPANEK
August, 1998
in "Celebrate Through Heartsongs" (Hyperion, 2002)

Music by
JOSEPH M. MARTIN (BMI)

31

time,_ a sign, of peace_ and grace and hap - pi -

ness; a sea-son of beau - ti - ful

rain - bows, a time for the heart_ to take flight. Cre -

HEARTSONGS

32

34

rea-son to look___ to the sky. O this was a sum - mer,___

rea-son to look___ to the sky.

___ a but - ter - fly sum - mer,___

This was a sum - mer,___ O

___ a time,___ a sign of

beau - ti - ful but - ter - fly, a time,___ a sign of

38

40

This was a sum - mer.
This was a sum - mer.
This was a sum - mer,
This was a sum - mer,
sum - mer.
sum - mer.

HEARTSONGS

Mattie wrote about many things including his observations about the natural world and what lessons and hidden beauties could be found there. For Mattie even the trees had a special Heartsong…

Poem: WHEN THE TREES SING
by Mattie J.T. Stepanek
May, 1998
in "Hope Through Heartsongs" (Hyperion, 2002)

When the trees sing,
It doesn't matter
If you know the song,
Or if you even know the words,
Or even if you know the tune.
What really matters is knowing
That trees are singing at all.

And then from later that year he wrote "Songs of the Wind."

Poem: SONGS OF THE WIND
by Mattie J.T. Stepanek
July, 1998
in "Hope Through Heartsongs" (Hyperion, 2002)

Listen to the wind.
If you listen carefully,
You will hear soft notes.
Listen with your mind and
Heart – you will hear a song.
A soft, relaxing song that
Reminds you of peace,
Harmony, and love.
If you hear this song,
Always remember it.
For if you do,
You can teach it
To other people,
And they, too, will forever
Remember the Heartsongs.

SONGS OF THE WIND

Words based on the poem
"Songs of the Wind" *by*
MATTIE J.T. STEPANEK
July, 1998
in "Hope Through Heartsongs" (Hyperion, 2002)

Words and music by
JOSEPH M. MARTIN (BMI)

-ten to the wind, lis - ten to the wind blow.

Lis - ten to the wind, lis - ten to the wind blow.

Lis-ten to the wind, lis - ten to the wind, lis - ten to the wind blow.

Ah

Ah

44

HEARTSONGS

Lyrics:

28 — care - ful - ly, ___ you can hear the mu - sic.

28 (lower voice) — You can hear the mu - sic.

31 / 32 — Lis - ten with your mind and heart ___ and

31 / 32 (lower voice) — *Oh* _____

34 — you will hear a song. *mf* The dance of

34 (lower voice) — You will hear a song. *mf* The dance of

46

wind and trees, re - mind - ing you of peace;

a song of har - mo - ny___ and___ love.___

Lis - ten to the wind, lis - ten to the wind, lis -

55
mf
dim. poco a poco al fine
Be still and lis - ten to the
mf
dim. poco a poco al fine
Be still and lis - ten to the
55
mf
dim. poco a poco al fine
58
16
48
60
with growing intensity
mp
cresc. poco a poco
wind.
Re - lax - ing
mp
cresc. poco a poco
wind.
Re - lax - ing
58
60
with growing intensity
mp
cresc. poco a poco
61
har - mo - ny sent from a - bove.
har - mo - ny sent from a - bove.
61

54

Oo

Oo

Lis - ten to the wind blow.

Lis - ten to the wind blow.

Lis - ten to the wind blow.

Lis - ten to the wind blow.

rit. poco a poco al fine

rit. poco a poco al fine

dim. poco a poco al fine

dim. poco a poco al fine

dim. poco a poco al fine

HEARTSONGS

One of Mattie's early poems celebrated the diversity of creation and taught us all a lesson in respect, tolerance and the miracle mosaic that is humankind.

Poem: SHADES OF LIFE
by Mattie J.T. Stepanek
January, 2002
in "Celebrate Through Heartsongs" (Hyperion, 2002)

The color of sky
Is blue and grays.
The color of earth
Is greens and browns.
The color of hope
Is rainbows and purple
And the color of peace
Is people, together.

Listen to Mattie's words from a poetic prayer he called "The Gift of Color."

Poem: THE GIFT OF COLOR
by Mattie J.T. Stepanek
January, 1995
in "Heartsongs" (Hyperion, 2002)

Thank You
For all the colors of the rainbow.
Thank You
For sharing these colors
With all of the fish
And all of the birds
And all of the flowers
That you have given us.
And thank You
For the colors of the
Heaven-in-the-earth
And of the
Heaven-in-the-sky,
And for sharing these colors
In the people of the world.
You give us color
As a gift, God,
And I thank You
For all of these
Beautiful colors and
Beautiful things and
Beautiful people.

A WORLD OF DIFFERENCE

Words by
JOSEPH M. MARTIN *and*
PAMELA STEWART (BMI)

Music by
JOSEPH M. MARTIN (BMI)

We're the col - ors of the rain - bow. We're the

We're the col - ors of the rain - bow. We're the

stars up in the sky. No two of us are quite the same, and

stars up in the sky. No two of us are quite the same, and

here's the rea - son why: we all have a pur - pose and a

here's the rea - son why: we all have a pur - pose and a

60

HEARTSONGS

64

dif-f'rence in our world;__ for it takes a world of dif-f'ren-ces___ to make a

dif-f'rence in our world;__ for it takes a world of dif-f'ren-ces___ to make a

dif - f'rence in our world._____

dif - f'rence in our world._____

As Mattie faced an uncertain future he remained hopeful. Through the eyes of faith he saw a better day. His poetry reflected a deep understanding of the journey of life. He wrote a short verse in December of 1998 that reflects some of his remarkable insight.

Poem: FACING THE FUTURE
by Mattie J.T. Stepanek
December, 1998
in "Hope Through Heartsongs" (Hyperion, 2002)

> *Every journey begins*
> *With but a small step.*
> *And every day is a chance*
> *For a new, small step*
> *In the right direction.*
> *Just follow your Heartsong.*

THE JOURNEY

from "Symphony in E minor"
by ANTONIN DVORAK (1841-1904)
and the Shaker hymn, SIMPLE GIFTS
Arranged by
JOSEPH M. MARTIN (BMI)

be in the val-ley of love and de - light. When

true sim-plic-i-ty is gained, to bow and to bend we___

shan't be a-shamed. To turn, turn will be___ our de-light 'til by

turn - ing, turn - ing we come out right.

70

HEARTSONGS

72

Even in face of his terrible disease Mattie remained hopeful about the future. His faith remained strong and on New Years Day 2003 he penned a challenge for us all in the form of inspiring resolution.

Poem: RESOLUTION BLESSING
by Mattie J.T. Stepanek
January, 2003
in "Reflections of a Peacemaker" (Andrews McMeel, 2005)

Let our breath be gentle wind,
Let our ears be of those who listen,
Let our hearts be not ones
That rage so quickly and
Thus blow dramatically,
And uselessly.
Let our spirits attend and be
Most diligent to the soft
Yet desperate whisper of
Hope and peace for our world.
Let our souls be those
Which watch for the Lord,
Waiting with wonder and want.
Let our eyes be attentive
With interest and respect,
Let our minds be committed
To health and happiness,
Let our hands join
In helpful resolution
To being our best person,
Praying and playing and
Passing through moments
Of pain or memory-
Makers of pleasure
Touching the future, together.

A HEARTSONG BLESSING

Words based on the posm
"Resolution Blessing" by
MATTIE J.T. STEPANEK
January, 2003
in "Reflections of a Peacemaker" (Andrews McMeel, 2005)

Music by
JOSEPH M. MARTIN (BMI)

Let our ears be of those who lis - ten. Let our hearts be love songs for the earth. Let all our spir - its serve, bring - ing hope and peace to all the world.

76

ness. Let our souls be filled with won -

PART I

der. Let us join our hands_____ in this

PART II

der. Let us join__ our__ hands_____ in this__

mo - ment._____ We are one in

mo - ment._____ We are one in

78

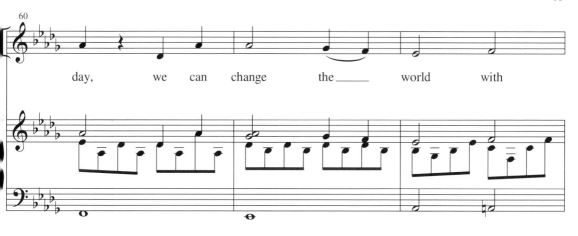

day,   we can change   the _____ world   with

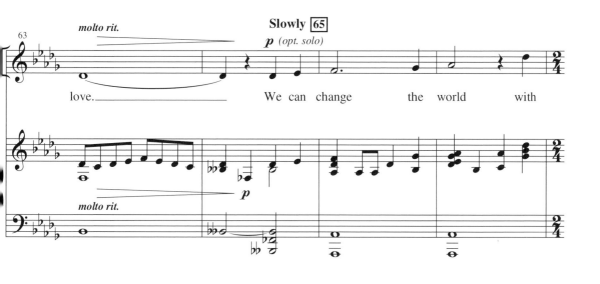

love._____ We can change   the world   with

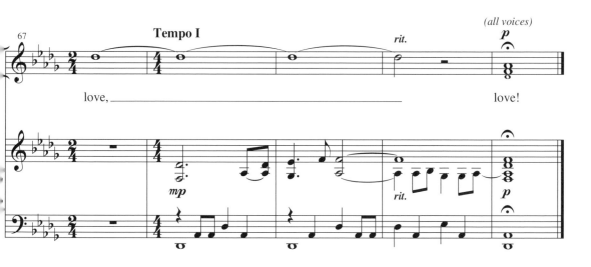

love,_____ love!

FINAL:

Mattie died on June 22nd, 2004. Through the music of his life he left us a great legacy of joy and grace. In his poetry he reminded us that we are community with each other, a mosaic of great beauty. He taught us, in his gentle way, that we were created to be a people of peace and children of hope.

In his final book, Mattie wrote: "We are each messengers called to bring hope and peace to others, who then may choose to become messengers for yet others, for the world, and for the future. May this simple message touch hearts and minds, spirits and lives, and inspire each member of humanity to make a gentle choice, and become a messenger of peace."

Poem: BELIEVING IN SOMEDAY
by Mattie J.T. Stepanek
August, 2000
in "Hope Through Heartsongs" (Hyperion, 2002)

Maybe,
Someday,
We will all join hands
And live together...
Helping each other,
Loving each other.
Maybe,
Someday,
We will all make the world
A much better place...
And be like a gigantic,
Smoothly rushing river of peace –
A loving circle that nothing can break.
Maybe,
Someday,
We may start with just one person,
And one permanent peace agreement
Within one's self, within one's world.
Personal peace can then spread
Within and between the families,
Then within and between communities,
And then within and around the whole world.
Maybe,
Someday,
We can become
As close to perfect
As anything and anyone can get.
Let us each join our own Heartsong
With this old song of the heart, and believe...
* "Let there be peace on earth,*
*   And let it begin with me."*

I BELIEVE IN SOMEDAY

Words based on the poem
"Believing in Someday" by
MATTIE J.T. STEPANEK
August, 2000
in "Hope Through Heartsongs" (Hyperion, 2002)

Music by
JOSEPH M. MARTIN (BMI)
Incorporating:
PEACE LIKE A RIVER
Traditional Spiritual

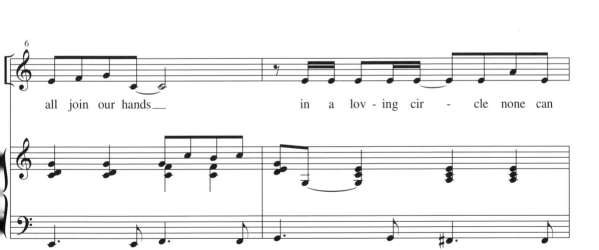

Words Copyright © 2002 by Mattie J.T. Stepanek
International Copyright Secured. All Rights Reserved.
Music Copyright © 2011 by HAL LEONARD - MILWIN MUSIC CORP.
International Copyright Secured. All Rights Reserved.

Some - day, we'll sing a song of peace.

Some - day, we'll sing a song of peace.

Come and learn the mel - o - dy.___

We can sing in har - mo - ny.___

mf *cresc. poco a poco*

We will make a ring - ing, sing - ing sym - pho - ny!

mf *cresc. poco a poco*

We will make a ring - ing, sing - ing sym - pho - ny!

mf *cresc. poco a poco*

88

Some - day, deep in my soul.____

peace like a riv - er in my soul. I've got

Some - day, yes, I be - lieve.__ I've got

peace like a riv - er. I've got peace like a riv - er. I've got

cresc.

peace like a riv - er in my soul.____ Makes me

cresc.

peace like a riv - er in my soul. Make me

90

92

HEARTSONG

Reprise

Words based on the poem
"Heartsong" *by*
MATTIE J.T. STEPANEK
March, 1996
in "Journey Through Heartsongs" (Hyperion, 2002)

Music by
JOSEPH M. MARTIN (BMI)

94